The Wild Guys

Rebecca Shaw and Andrew Wreggitt began writing plays together in 1991. Rebecca has been a professional advertising and video script writer for sixteen years and Andrew is an award-winning playwright and screenwriter. Together, they recently received the Solange Karsh Award for best play in the 1992 National Playwrighting Competition for *The Wild Guys*. Rebecca and Andrew have also penned *Ms Lone Pine* and *Two-Step*, the final play in their *Lone Pine Trilogy*. They are married and live in Calgary.

The Wild Guys

by Andrew Wreggitt
& Rebecca Shaw

Blizzard Publishing • Winnipeg

The Wild Guys first published 1994 by
Blizzard Publishing Inc.
301–89 Princess St., Winnipeg, Canada R3B 1K6
© 1993 Andrew Wreggitt and Rebecca Shaw

Cover art by Linda Mullin.
Printed in Canada by Kromar Printing Ltd.

Published with the assistance of
the Canada Council and the Manitoba Arts Council.

Caution

This play is fully protected under the copyright laws of Canada and all other countries of the Copyright Union and is subject to royalty. Except in the case of brief passages quoted in a review of this book, no part of this publication (including cover design) may be reproduced or transmitted in any form, by any means, electronic or mechanical, including recording and information storage and retrieval systems, without permission in writing from the publisher, or, in the case of photocopying or other reprographic copying, without a licence from Canadian Reprography Collective (CANCOPY).

Rights to produce, in whole or part, by any group, amateur or professional, are retained by the authors.

"Keep walking, though there's no place to get to" originally published in *Unseen Rain, Quatrains of Rumi* by John Moyne and Coleman Barks, Threshold Books, 1986. Reprinted by permission.

"Heart of Gold" by Neil Young, © 1971, 1972 Silver Fiddle, all rights reserved. Reprinted by permission.

Canadian Cataloguing in Publication Data

Wreggitt, Andrew, 1955–
   The wild guys
   A play.
   ISBN 0-921368-37-2
I. Shaw, Rebecca, 1954–   II. Title.
PS8595.R44W5 1994   C812'.54   C94-920034-4
PR9199.3.W74W5 1994

The Wild Guys was commissioned by Stage One, The Petro-Canada Plays. The one-act version premièred September 28, 1992, at Lunchbox Theatre, Calgary, with the following cast:

STEWART	Daryl Shuttleworth
ANDY	Vince Metcalfe
RANDALL	Howard Siegel
ROBIN	David LeReaney

Directed by Margaret Bard
Set Design by Tracy Nunnally
Lighting Design by Steve Isom
Costumes by Hal Kerbes
Stage Manager: Donna Sharpe

The full-length version of *The Wild Guys* premièred at the Arts Club Theatre, Vancouver, on May 25, 1993, with the following cast:

STEWART	Jackson Davies
ANDY	Vince Metcalfe
RANDALL	Howard Siegel
ROBIN	Hrothgar Mathews

Directed by Margaret Bard
Set Design by Ted Roberts
Lighting Design by Marsha Sibthorpe
Costumes by Pearl Bellesen
Stage Manager: Caryn Fehr
Assistant Stage Manager: John James Hong

The full-length script of the *The Wild Guys* was premièred in eastern Canada at Lighthouse Festival Theatre, Port Dover, Ontario, on July 27, 1993.

Special thanks to Margaret Bard, Bartley Bard, Jackson Davies, Bill Millerd and Warren Ham.

Characters

STEWART: Stewart Gyver, about 40, the manager of the Super Food Mart grocery store in the tiny northern Alberta town of Lone Pine.

ANDY: Andy Graham, 50 years old, an executive at Super Food Mart's head office in the city and a member of a men's group.

RANDALL: Randall Harrison, a very fit and polished forty-year-old, a lawyer in the city firm that handles the Super Food Mart account.

ROBIN: Robin Cunningham, 38ish, a member of the same men's group that Andy Graham belongs to.

Setting

Everything except Scene One takes place somewhere in the bush outside the tiny northern town of Lone Pine. On stage, the bush country is represented in a very simple way: essentially the stage is bare, with a few trees, big rocks and bushes that are rearranged between scenes to show the men's progression.

The time is Summer, the present.

A note on the production

The Wild Guys is a comedy, but the essence of the humour lies in the absolute sincerity of each of the characters. These are middle-aged, heterosexual men who are confused by where life has taken them and are in need of some answers—any answers. The play is at its funniest and most touching when it is played straight—"in spite of the laughter of the audience" as Margaret Bard once put it.

Geographical references and names of towns can be adjusted to suit the location of the production. Likewise, "Super Food Mart" might be changed to the name of a local grocery store, if preferred.

Music references are suggestions only and the responsibility for securing music rights belongs with the producers of the play.

Act One

Scene One

(Spotlights come up one at a time on the heads and shoulders of the four wild guys, all of whom are on the telephone. STEWART is in a grocer's apron. ANDY has a tie and jacket on. RANDALL has on a white shirt, tie askew. ROBIN is wearing a collarless shirt and a leather thong around his neck with an animal claw of some kind dangling from it.)

STEWART: Maxie, it's me. Listen, great news! I just got a call from Andy Graham, the guy from head office? … Yeah, yeah, the big honcho who was so impressed with Hawaiian Krazy Daze. He wants me to go with him on a guys' weekend kinda thing. It can only mean he wants to talk promotion …

ANDY: Yes, Barbara Graham please. It's Mr. Graham … her husband. … Well, ask her to step out of her meeting, please.

STEWART: You know, maybe a bigger outlet … wouldn't that be something? Life in the big city? … I dunno. Airdie, Westaskiwin … who knows …

ANDY: Hi, Barbara, it's me … I just wanted to remind you that I'm taking some guys out on a weekend men's retreat today … Well, in that case I probably won't see you before I go. We're driving up tonight and starting out for the lake early tomorrow morning … Randall, Robin and a fellow from our store in Lone Pine … Yes, the same guy who came up with that bizarre Hawaiian promotion …

RANDALL: Hi, Tammy … Bad news, kitten. I can't make it this weekend … I know I did … Tammy, believe me there's nothing in the world I would love more than to do the triathlon with you … I know … and I feel terrible about it. But I totally forgot that I promised Andy I'd go on this men's sensitivity weekend with him …

ROBIN: Mrs. Filbert? ... Hi there, it's Robin ...

RANDALL: Andy Graham. He's a very important client, a top executive at the Super Food Mart and he's really into that shit ...

ROBIN: Robin Cunningham from the Eco-Store? ... Oh, I'm fine, dear, how are you? ... That's a shame ... uh huh ... listen, the reason I was ... uh huh ... I know, what can you do? Cats just go wherever they want to, don't they? Listen, the reason I was calling was I promised I'd sit with you at the recycling bin on Saturday ... no, no this Saturday. Anyway, I can't make it. This wonderful opportunity has come up. One of the guys from my local men's group is going to take a few of us out on a soul exploration weekend.

STEWART: Aw, you know. Drink a few beers, fish a little. He's bringin' a coupla his pals from the city. I'm taking them up to Zippermouth Lake.

ROBIN: You know, men rediscovering their primal natures in the forest, a chance to feel our kinship with stone, water, fire, tree ...

ANDY: What's Danny up to this weekend?

ROBIN: No, the forest, Mrs. Filbert, not the florist ...

ANDY: Well, maybe you should keep an eye on him ... Yes, I remember what Linda said about trust ...

RANDALL: I know it's not very far but there's an older guy coming along ...

ANDY: All weekend? Why are you meeting on the weekend?

(Their voices begin to overlap.)

ROBIN: I know. Bus passes are way too expensive in this city ... Listen, I've gotta go, Mrs. Filbert ...

STEWART: I know. A few beers, that's all. I gotta go.

ANDY: Then I'll see you Sunday night, *after* your meeting.

RANDALL: Right. Kisses. Good luck this weekend.

ROBIN: Bye.

STEWART: Bye.

ANDY: Bye.

RANDALL: Bye.

ALL: Jesus!

(Blackout. Suggested music: Paul Simon's "Obvious Child.")

Scene Two

(As the music continues, lights come up slowly and rosy, in imitation of the rising sun. On stage are a few trees and several large rocks suggesting the bush country.

STEWART enters. He wears a worn and bulging backpack that clinks mysteriously. He is followed by an enthusiastic, but exhausted, ROBIN, whose own extra-large backpack has a deerskin drum and guitar tied to it. Next comes RANDALL, still looking fresh and fit ... then ANDY brings up the rear. The men walk single file across the stage and exit. A long pause.

Music fades.

STEWART re-enters, followed by ROBIN, RANDALL and ANDY. They continue walking in the same line.)

RANDALL: Hey, uhh ... Stewart?

(STEWART turns and they all stop. ROBIN immediately throws himself down to rest.)

STEWART: Yeah?

RANDALL: We were just here.

STEWART: *(Looking around, a little confused, then lies.)* Yeah. I was gonna take us on a short cut, but I decided against it.

ROBIN: Can we rest for awhile?

RANDALL: If it's five miles in to this lake ... *(Checks his watch.)* It's been two hours of bushwhacking ... We should be getting close.

STEWART: *(Still looking around.)* Oh, yeah. We're close, very close.

ROBIN: God, it's wonderful, isn't it? I can already feel the primal blood starting to course through my veins!

ANDY: Smell that fresh mountain air! You know, in Dr. Rothenberg's new book he says that it's important to physically remove yourself from the source of your stress in order to begin some kind of healing process.

ROBIN: That is so true!

RANDALL: *(To STEWART.)* You'd tell us if you thought you might be lost, right?

STEWART: *(Laughs a little too heartily.)* Lost! We're not lost ... my God, I grew up out here. *(Realizes something.)* Not that I wouldn't consider moving. I mean, if the right opportunity came up ...

RANDALL: And this lake, this Zippermouth Lake, you've been there, right?

STEWART: Well, not me personally, but I got real clear directions from my buddy Rick. The fishing's supposed to be fantastic. You know, that's why they call it Zippermouth Lake. Only about five guys know about it. You don't want lots of people making a trail in here and fishing the lake out.

RANDALL: No, we wouldn't want to have a trail to follow.

ROBIN: I feel good, you know? Whooo! The city just beats the masculinity out of a guy, but out here you can feel the warrior standing up in you, the wildman starting to stalk back there in the old subconscious ... You know what I'm thinking? I'm thinking why don't we start doing some body work? I mean, let's get right into it.

(As ROBIN talks, STEWART starts unloading beer bottles from his pack.)

STEWART: *(Looking up.)* My brother does body work. He has a shop in Red Deer.

ROBIN: That's not the kind of body work I meant.

STEWART: Anybody want a beer?

RANDALL: It's eight-thirty in the morning, Stew.

STEWART: *(Cracking a beer.)* Yeah, time's a wastin'.

(STEWART offers the beer around but gets no takers. He shrugs and takes a long pull himself.)

ROBIN: I'm talking about physically preparing the body for a spiritual journey. Meditation, Chi self-massage ... Do you know what I'm talking about?

STEWART: *(Snorts.)* Self-massage ... yeah, right.

ROBIN: We do it every week.

STEWART: Yeah, who doesn't, eh?

ROBIN: In our group, before every meeting.

STEWART: You do it ... together?

ANDY: Stewart, Robin is talking about a Taoist form of mental and physical relaxation. Like rubbing your kneecap a certain way, or the back of your neck ...

STEWART: *(The light comes on.)* Ohhh ...

ANDY: I want to do a full body work session, too, Robin, but maybe we should wait until we get to the cabin …

ROBIN: It's just that the weekend is so short. You know, a little meditation might ease us through the transition we're making as we physically pass from the desensitized world of civilized man to the hyper-sensitive world of forest man.

STEWART: What?

ROBIN: Just a quick centring exercise, Andy?

ANDY: Well, if that's all right with everyone else. Randall?

RANDALL: Sure, why not? Maybe "forest man" over there will figure out where we are.

(ANDY sits cross-legged on the ground and ROBIN and RANDALL both imitate the position. They begin to relax. STEWART looks on in confusion. He starts to edge away.)

ANDY: Stewart, you'll join us, won't you?

STEWART: You know, I thought maybe we'd have a few beers, a few yuks, you know, but like I don't know anything about this stuff you're talking about …

ROBIN: Oh, for heaven's sake! It's meditation. It's not that difficult a concept to grasp. It's about using your brain.

ANDY: Come on, Stewart, try it. You might be pleasantly surprised by the experience.

(STEWART reluctantly assumes the position.)

ANDY: Okay, everyone, eyes closed … Now breathe in deeply … and out. Breathe in … and out …

STEWART: This isn't some sort of weird cult, is it?

ROBIN: Oh, sweet Jesus!

STEWART: … 'cause like I'm Presbyterian, eh?

ANDY: No, it's not. Just relax, Stewart. Breathe in … Start to feel the earth's energy being drawn up through you … and out. You're like a tree with roots … up from the centre of the earth, through your buttocks …

(STEWART's eyes pop open.)

and into your lungs and out through the top of your head. Breathe in …

(STEWART closes his eyes again and takes a swig of beer.)

and out. Breathe in …

(STEWART *takes another swig of beer.*)

and out. Can you hear the Chi beginning to move in you like a wind, awakening your heart and lungs and liver and …

STEWART: I can hear my stomach.

ROBIN: Oh, God! This is hopeless!

STEWART: Well, I'm hungry.

ANDY: Maybe we should wait until we're at the cabin and we're a little more comfortable with each other. *(Gets up and goes over to STEWART.)* I'm sorry, Stewart, I guess I didn't explain very clearly the nature of this weekend.

STEWART: No, no, look, I don't want to put a damper on things … I'm as hip as the next guy, you know. I just thought when you said a guys' weekend you meant … you know …

ROBIN: Drinking and throwing up?

STEWART: *(Tentatively.)* Yeah.

ANDY: It's a different sort of guys' weekend, Stewart. Let me try and explain. A couple of years ago, I realized that my lifestyle had left me isolated, without many real male friends. I had achieved "success" in my personal and professional life, but I still felt that something was missing. I began to attend a regular men's meeting, just a study group really, but I was fascinated by getting to know this diverse new network of men.

STEWART: Network?

ANDY: Weekends like this are about men talking to men. Really talking.

STEWART: You mean about work? Like jobs? Promotions and stuff?

ANDY: Yes, but not just that. We also talk about how we feel. What drives us, what makes us feel sad, or fulfilled …

RANDALL: Well, I'm with Stewart. What I feel is hungry.

STEWART: Yeah! I'm starved. Where's those cheezies, Rob?

ROBIN: My name is not Rob, it's Robin.

STEWART: Right. Whatever. C'mon. Cheezies.

(ROBIN *doesn't move to open his pack.*)

RANDALL: Robin … all the food's in your pack. Let's go.

ROBIN: *(Pauses.)* Well, I didn't want to spoil the surprise, but I guess I have to. *(Beat.)* I didn't bring any food.

RANDALL: Ahuh. That's very funny, Robin. Now make with the cheezies, okay?

ROBIN: Don't you see? This is the perfect way to draw the wildman out of us. We spend a weekend hunting and gathering, like countless generations before us, back to the dawn of time itself.

ANDY: This is something we should have discussed as a group, Robin.

STEWART: Jesus! All I brought was beer!

ROBIN: We can smear the blood of our prey on our faces, become one with the spirits of the forest.

RANDALL: Our prey? I don't know about the rest of you, but when I get hungry, I get cranky.

ROBIN: It's all the stress of your city life. The body work will help with that …

RANDALL: I can think of one kind of body work that might help.

(RANDALL moves toward ROBIN menacingly.)

ROBIN: *(Delighted.)* See? Already, the primal male aggression is asserting itself. *(He hugs RANDALL.)* Whoo! This is gonna be a great weekend!

(Blackout. Suggested music: "Wild Thing.")

Scene Three

(Lights up to reveal a slightly different arrangement of trees and rocks. It is now midday. RANDALL, ROBIN and ANDY kneel down stage centre, looking over the edge of the stage. Music fades. RANDALL holds a string over the edge; a safety pin is attached to the end. They are fishing.)

ROBIN: *(Whispers.)* There! There's a big one!

ANDY: *(Whispers.)* He's coming closer … hold it steady now …

ROBIN: Don't you think you should jig it up and down a little?

RANDALL: I will … shhh … come on you beauty … bite that safety pin …

(STEWART enters, zipping up his fly. He looks around and casually picks up ROBIN's guitar. He thinks for a minute, then hammers out the first few chords of an old rock and roll song. He's not very good. RANDALL, ROBIN and ANDY leap about a foot in surprise.)

STEWART notices his audience is not totally enraptured by the song. He puts the guitar down a little guiltily. RANDALL yanks the string back petulantly.)

STEWART: Uhh ... sorry.

RANDALL: Great! We find the one fish in this whole creek and our fearless local guide decides to give a concert.

ROBIN: I know we lost the fish, but look how we were pulling together, striving toward our common cause ...

RANDALL: Don't start with that shit, Robin. If it hadn't been for you we'd be having a pleasant hike instead of rooting around for something to eat like a gang of yuppie hoboes! On top of that *(Points a finger at STEWART.)* I don't think he knows where he's going, Andy.

STEWART: Sure I do. We're almost there. We go through this rock slide, then around the shoulder of that mountain and it's right there. *(RANDALL just looks at him.)* Honest.

ANDY: It's interesting, isn't it, how the lack of food brings out our more aggressive side.

ROBIN: *(Nods towards RANDALL.)* He's so goal-oriented.

RANDALL: *(Looks at ROBIN.)* It's not as though I haven't been provoked.

ANDY: I understand. It's natural. Men are often in situations where they have strong feelings. But usually social convention requires us to hide them. That's one thing a weekend like this tries to achieve. We try to reach those emotions riding just below the surface. Anger, fear, grief, loneliness ...

RANDALL: Look, all I want is a cheeseburger.

ROBIN: *(Gleefully.)* But you can't have one and that's the point!

ANDY: *(To RANDALL.)* How do you normally express anger?

RANDALL: I beat the crap out of someone on the squash court.

ANDY: And you shake hands at the end but the source of your anger goes unexpressed.

RANDALL: I was kidding, Andy.

ANDY: It may come out in the way you pursue a legal case, or in the way you drive home ... or worst of all, and I'm not saying you do this, but we often take our anger out on the people we love.

RANDALL: You're talking about some kind of vague, generic anger here, Andy. Anger about what?

ANDY: It's difficult to know what the anger's really about. Look, I'm not a psychologist but it's something we all grapple with in our own way. The expression of anger has been socialized out of us, but what do we do with that energy?

ROBIN: *(Eagerly, over ANDY.)* We transfer it.

ANDY: We transfer it.

RANDALL: I think it was a rhetorical question, Robin.

ROBIN: *(Butting in.)* You say you're angry about the lack of food, but really you're angry at your absent father. You're furious that he didn't initiate you into the world of men, that you were robbed of your mythopoetic heritage …

RANDALL: *(Turns to ANDY.)* Look, I agreed to come along on this weekend but I'm not crazy about Dr. Freud over here playing clinical psychologist on me.

ROBIN: Still hanging on to that macho resistance …

RANDALL: Especially when Dr. Freud wants to smear blood on his face and dance around a fire.

STEWART: We're not actually gonna do that, are we?

ANDY: Randall, you came on this weekend to indulge me, right? Important client, you didn't want to turn me down.

RANDALL: No, it's not like that.

ANDY: But you know deep down you wouldn't have lost me as a client. You also came for another reason, didn't you?

RANDALL: Well, it sounded like this was going to be fun.

ANDY: But is fun a means or an end?

RANDALL: Does it matter?

ANDY: Why did you come?

RANDALL: Okay. My girlfriend wanted me to go on a triathlon.

STEWART: Jesus, really?

RANDALL: She's twenty-two.

STEWART: Twenty-two?

RANDALL: I mean, every weekend it's something else, you know? Scuba diving, mountain biking, wind-surfing. Shit, a triathlon!

STEWART: *(Wistfully.)* Twenty-two.

RANDALL: All I could think was, great, here's one I won't have to do.

I was looking forward to relaxing and healing up. I was hoping for bacon and eggs, steaks fried in butter, baked potatoes and sour cream …

ROBIN: What is that? Quest for cholesterol?

RANDALL: I'm thirty-nine years old. It's tough to hold down a job and keep up with her …

ANDY: Why do you have to keep up?

RANDALL: Because if I don't, I'll lose her.

ROBIN: Wait! Wait! I just remembered. *(Digs in his pack and pulls out a crystal.)* I brought the talking crystal. I went to an anger workshop last year at Mendecino and the talking crystal really helped.

STEWART: A talking crystal?

ROBIN: The idea is, the speaker holds the crystal and as long as he holds it, no one interrupts. Then you pass it on. After awhile, I swear the thing gets hot to hold, it's so full of psychic energy.

ANDY: We're already talking, Robin.

ROBIN: Yeah, but we didn't ritualize the space first …

STEWART: *(Takes the crystal from ROBIN.)* Whoa! That's some rock!

ANDY: *(Back to RANDALL.)* I thought you were seeing someone in your firm.

RANDALL: Judith. Yeah, well, that didn't turn out to be a very good idea. I think we were too similar.

ANDY: In age?

RANDALL: A little below the belt there, Andy.

ANDY: Exactly.

ROBIN: It's a classic. Fear of mortality. You keep getting older but your girlfriends stay the same age.

RANDALL: There's nothing wrong with a little fear of mortality, know what I mean, Robin?

STEWART: *(Laughs.)* Below the belt. Hah.

ANDY: I understand the stress of the legal profession can be very hard on relationships.

RANDALL: Yeah. Well, maybe we should keep looking for this cabin. So we have a little more time for hunting and gathering.

(They all stand up and start to pull on their packs.)

STEWART: *(Still admiring the crystal.)* So where did you find this rock anyway?

ROBIN: Birks.

(Blackout. Suggested music: "Born To Be Wild" by Steppenwolf.)

Scene Four

(Lights up; it is still midday. The moveable scenery has been altered again. Music fades. Enter the four intrepid hikers, filing wearily across the stage in this order: STEWART, ROBIN, ANDY, RANDALL.)

ROBIN: *(As he walks.)* I can't believe you did that!

RANDALL: Look, Robin, he's been saying he's sorry for two hours. Can't you just drop it?

(The wild guys file off. Long beat. They come back on in the same order.)

ROBIN: Cost me four hundred and fifty bucks.

(STEWART stops and the line bumps to a stop behind him.)

STEWART: I just put it down, you know, to take a pee …

ROBIN: Oh sure, he puts down a four-hundred-and-fifty-dollar crystal on a scree slope.

STEWART: Well, it's a bunch of rocks. They all look the same!

ANDY: We lost a whole hour looking for that crystal. Maybe we could cut our losses here.

ROBIN: I had a lot of psychic energy invested in that thing.

RANDALL: It's a rock! A rock! If you paid four hundred and fifty bucks for it, that's your fault! Stop whining! God! I'd go home if I knew where the hell I was!

(RANDALL yanks a beer out of STEWART's pack for himself.)

ROBIN: *(Petulantly.)* Robert Bly held that crystal once.

ANDY: Look, Robin, Stewart has apologized. Be gracious about it. Put it behind you.

(STEWART notices something on the ground ahead of him. He kneels down hunter-tracker style to examine it.)

STEWART: Hey … What's this?

ROBIN: What?

STEWART: *(Smiles, pleased.)* Well, that's it. The cabin's just up here.

RANDALL: Yeah? What makes you so sure?

STEWART: It's obvious, isn't it? I mean, these are the tracks of the last guys to go up there.

(The guys go over and examine the tracks.)

RANDALL: That's a good sign. At least we're not alone out here.

STEWART: I told you I knew where I was going. I suppose you city guys just get a little nervous when you lose sight of a highrise.

ANDY: They can't be more than a day or two old ...

STEWART: You guys are gonna love this cabin. It's got everything in it, fishing rods, a nice little wood stove ...

ANDY: Holy smokes, look at the size of this guy's feet!

ROBIN: They look like snowshoes.

(STEWART comes over to look.)

STEWART: Yeah, those are real boats, aren't they? *(STEWART fits his boot into the track.)* Must be size twelve and a halfs.

(They all look at STEWART's foot. The boot is a perfect fit. ANDY, RANDALL, and ROBIN put their feet into the other tracks in comparison.)

ANDY: Oh, for God's sake!

ROBIN: Stewart!

RANDALL: These are our tracks!!!

ROBIN: You mean we've been going in circles all this time?

RANDALL: *(To STEWART.)* You're lost.

STEWART: Am not.

RANDALL: You are too! Admit it!

STEWART: No.

RANDALL: *(To the others.)* He's lost. So are we. We don't have any food, we don't have a tent ...

ROBIN: Or a crystal.

RANDALL: ... and what if it gets dark before we find this cabin?

STEWART: Maybe I took us, sorta the long way around but ... *(RANDALL laughs.)* but we're not exactly lost.

RANDALL: How could we be more "exactly" lost? In what possible, hypothetical way could we be more thoroughly or precisely lost? In your opinion.

STEWART: *(Looks at ANDY.)* He's a lawyer, isn't he?

>*(RANDALL stalks off. STEWART looks over at ROBIN who also turns his back.)*

Okay. So we're kinda lost.

>*(The other guys all groan.)*

The lake shoulda been back there. I dunno. Rick's directions were a little vague.

ANDY: You didn't feel you could share that with us earlier? When we might have been able to help?

STEWART: Wellll … You know … I didn't want you guys to think …

ROBIN: What? That you have the wilderness instincts of my neighbour's Shitzu?

STEWART: Come on. It's gotta be around here somewhere.

>*(STEWART leads the three others off in the same single file. Blackout. Suggested music: "Born To Be Wild.")*

Scene Five

>*(Lights up. The stage is now predominantly rocks. The four wild guys walk on in single file along the very edge of the stage as if along a high rocky ledge. They're all a bit nervous but RANDALL is positively terror-stricken as he shuffles along sideways, his back against a rock wall. Music fades.)*

RANDALL: I'm telling you, Stewart, it's getting narrower!

STEWART: We just have to get around this shoulder and then it's a straight drop down to the valley.

RANDALL: *(Groans.)* Oh, God, don't say it like that! *(Turns, appealing to ANDY.)* I don't think we should go any farther …

ANDY: It'll be all right.

STEWART: We have to keep going.

RANDALL: I've read about things like this. They're called terrain traps. You walk in all right, but then you can't get out.

ANDY: Come on, Randall. We'll go a little farther and see where this takes us.

RANDALL: He's already told us where it takes us. We crawl along this cliff face until we fall off and drop into the valley!

ROBIN: Well, we can't just stop here. We have to keep going.

RANDALL: *(Stubbornly.)* No. No, I'm not going any farther.

STEWART: You know what I think?

RANDALL: What?

STEWART: I think you're scared.

RANDALL: Scared?

STEWART: Yeah. Scared.

RANDALL: Well, I'm not.

STEWART: Oh, right. So, what's the problem then?

ROBIN: *(Interested.)* Yeah, Randall, what is it?

RANDALL: I just have a thing about heights, that's all.

STEWART: *(Laughs.)* What? You think you're gonna fall off and go splat down there on those rocks?

RANDALL: *(Groans.)* Splat?

ANDY: It's a matter of perception, Randall. This ledge is easily, what? six feet wide, maybe more?

(STEWART stands at the very edge and pretends to teeter there.)

STEWART: Whoa, whoa, whoa …

RANDALL: Oh, for God's sake, Stewart, stop clowning around.

ANDY: Imagine a six-foot-wide hallway in your office building. Do you think you could walk down that hallway without bumping into the walls?

RANDALL: Of course I could.

ANDY: In fact, most hallways are only about four feet wide. A hallway this wide would seem a luxury of open space in most office buildings.

STEWART: *(Looking over the edge, teasing.)* I wonder how long before you'd hit bottom.

ANDY: Just imagine you're going down a wide hallway at work …

RANDALL: Right. With a five-hundred-foot drop to my left, a potential rock slide to my right and Jethro Bodine for a guide.

STEWART: You'd probably have time to write your will on the way down.

ROBIN: If you can visualize yourself doing something, you can accomplish it. All you have to do is close your eyes and picture yourself ...

RANDALL: I am not closing my eyes!

ANDY: Fear is something that's constructed in your own mind, a perception of danger even when none exists ...

RANDALL: None exists? What do you call falling five hundred feet and being dashed to pieces?

ANDY: ... and, by the same process, fear can be deconstructed as well.

RANDALL: God! This would be just too ironic!

ROBIN: What?

RANDALL: To die falling off a mountain on a men's sensitivity weekend. If my father were here, he'd be laughing his head off.

ANDY: No one's going to fall, Randall. But I am interested in the connection you make between your fear of heights and your father ...

ROBIN: Yeah.

RANDALL: Do you think this is an appropriate topic under the circumstances?

ROBIN: Come on, Randall. It's better if you can talk about it.

STEWART: *(Smugly.)* Yeah. The ones who aren't scared can help the ones who are.

RANDALL: *(Takes a step toward STEWART.)* It would almost be worth it to ...

STEWART: Oh look, he moved. Maybe this means we're ready to go.

ANDY: How about it, Randall?

RANDALL: Okay. Okay. Let's just go slowly, all right?

STEWART: Great. We're ready. Finally.

(STEWART turns, takes one step, stumbles and falls off the stage.)

Aaaaa ...

ROBIN, RANDALL and ANDY: Stewart!!!!

(Blackout.)

Scene Six

(Lights up. STEWART is off stage. ANDY and ROBIN are on their stomachs looking over the edge of the stage, where he fell. RANDALL still has his back against the wall and is petrified.)

RANDALL: Can you see him?

ANDY: Stewart?

STEWART: *(Off, from far away.)* Heeelp.

RANDALL: You're kidding! He's alive?!!

ANDY: He's on another ledge about thirty feet down.

STEWART: Heeelp.

ROBIN: Stewart, are you all right?

STEWART: Yeah, I think so.

ANDY: Are you sure? Check your ankles for fractures or sprains ...

STEWART: I'm okay. Just get me outta here!

ANDY: Find something solid to hang onto. And don't move.

(ANDY and ROBIN straighten up.)

ROBIN: Rope. We need a rope.

RANDALL: Don't look at me. I didn't think we'd be climbing K2 this weekend.

ROBIN: Andy?

ANDY: I didn't bring one either.

RANDALL: What are we gonna do?

ROBIN: I know! We could take off our bootlaces and tie them together.

RANDALL: You want to dangle a hundred-and-eighty-pound man over a gorge with our bootlaces?

ROBIN: Or we could tie our clothing together and make a rope like that. No, no ... I've seen it in a movie. It'll work. *(Starts to take off his jacket.)*

RANDALL: Look, even if we make a rope long enough, Stewart will start climbing it and pull us all over the edge.

ANDY: Randall's right. Even if we could hold him, he might lose his grip and fall.

RANDALL: At best, he'd be killed. At worst, he'd be maimed for life and sue the last nickel out of all of us.

ROBIN: I can't believe you're talking about money at a time like this.

STEWART: Andeeee! What's going on up there?

ANDY: It's okay, Stewart. We're working on it.

ROBIN: *(Lowers his voice.)* Well, we can't just leave him there!

ANDY: It's too dangerous to try and pull him up without proper equipment. We need help.

RANDALL: Right. Let's go back and get help.

ROBIN: We're lost. It could take days to find our way out of here.

STEWART: *(A little plaintively.)* You guuuuysss … what are you doing?

(ROBIN goes to the edge on all fours and looks over.)

ROBIN: Don't worry, Stewart. We'll get you out.

RANDALL: What's he doing?

ROBIN: *(Coming back to the others.)* Having a beer.

ANDY: We can't leave him alone on that ledge.

RANDALL: Right. Robin, you stay behind. Andy and I'll go for help.

ROBIN: Me? Why me? I don't think we should split up the group.

ANDY: If we don't, what will we do? I mean, we're stuck. This becomes quite a moral problem, doesn't it?

ROBIN: It does?

STEWART: Guuuyyysss …

ANDY: Our natural urge is to stay and comfort Stewart, but in the end, is that really the best decision?

RANDALL: Yeah, I don't know if waiting here for a rescue party to find us is such a good idea. I mean, who knows where he's brought us.

ROBIN: Not him, that's for sure.

ANDY: If we try to save him ourselves, we become culpable if our attempts result in harm. On the other hand, if we go in search of help and something happens to him while we're gone … well, either way, there is a certain complicity for us in whatever happens.

RANDALL: It's true. You can be sued for taking action or for not taking action.

STEWART: *(Fainter.)* Guuuyyysss …

ROBIN: But you're talking about this as though it's a negative thing.

RANDALL: You don't think that Stewart falling off a cliff is a negative thing?

ROBIN: Of course it is. What I mean is, accepting responsibility for each other in a group setting is not negative. It's empowering …

RANDALL: I hate that word.

ROBIN: Well, it is! It empowers each member of the group. That's the problem with modern society. We've forgotten how to be tribal.

RANDALL: That's ridiculous. Tribal societies were superstitious and gruesomely violent.

ANDY: Not all of them, Randall.

RANDALL: Okay, but most of them were.

ANDY: Take the Hopi culture in the American Southwest, for example …

RANDALL: Do you think we could get back to the topic here? What are we going to do about Stewart?

ROBIN: Well, maybe we should ask him. After all, he's the one most directly involved.

ANDY: That's a good idea.

RANDALL: Yeah, good thinking, Robin. Maybe we can get him to sign a waiver or something.

> *(ROBIN looks at RANDALL, disgusted. ANDY goes to the edge on all fours and looks over.)*

ANDY: *(Softly.)* Oh, my God!

ROBIN: What is it?

ANDY: He's gone.

ROBIN: What?!

> *(ROBIN rushes over to the ledge and looks over.)*

RANDALL: How can he be gone? Gone where …? *(The implication sinks in.)*

> *(ROBIN straightens up slowly.)*

ROBIN: Oh, my God.

RANDALL: *(Sinks to a sitting position.)* Oh, shit …

ROBIN: *(Full of remorse.)* It's our fault, you know? We should have done something. We're all responsible … each of us!

> *(A single hand comes out of the wings and STEWART pulls himself on stage as if pulling himself back up on the ledge. In his other hand, he has a half-finished beer.)*

STEWART: *(Sarcastically.)* Well, thanks for the help, you guys.

ANDY: Stewart!

STEWART: You shoulda seen when I opened this beer. Kabloowee! They really got shook up on the way down.

RANDALL: How did you …?

STEWART: I followed the ledge around and it led back up here.

ROBIN: Thank God you're all right!

ANDY: You just walked back up here?

STEWART: Yeah. No big deal.

RANDALL: *(Recovered enough to be angry.)* No big deal? Well, you could have told us what you were doing, for God's sake!

ANDY: Did it occur to you that we were worried?

ROBIN: Yeah! Do you have any idea what we were going through up here?! We're all in this together, you know. You could have said something!

STEWART: Well, it's not that easy to get your attention, know what I mean? *(Pause.)* Anyway, I found another way down, Andy. We're all set. I think I figured out where the lake is. We were in the wrong valley, that's all. We'll be tucked into the cabin in less than an hour. Guarantee it.

(The wild guys stand up and start to follow STEWART.)

RANDALL: The wrong valley. *(To ROBIN.)* We should have tried the bootlace thing.

(Blackout. Suggested music: Theme song from "The Good, the Bad and the Ugly.")

Scene Seven

(Lights up on a new arrangement of rocks and trees. Music fades. RANDALL, ANDY and ROBIN are sitting by their packs engaged in a heated debate. STEWART's pack is on stage but there is no sign of STEWART. All three men have their boots off and they are applying bandaids and moleskin to the blisters on their bare feet. They are also swatting at mosquitoes.)

RANDALL: I don't know how you can say that! He's a creation of the fifties.

ANDY: Not at all. He's a very typical modern man.

ROBIN: I know we laugh at him, but really he's more sad than anything.

RANDALL: Oh, for God's sake!

ANDY: Well, what would you say about a guy who is so alienated by his job that he's late for work every morning? It takes the cooperation of his entire household just to get the poor man out the door.

ROBIN: But he can't change the downward spiralling pattern of father-provider.

RANDALL: Okay, so he's got a few problems.

ANDY: More than just a few problems. He's a study in powerlessness.

ROBIN: A man whose unconscious needs are at war with the life he's trying to lead.

ANDY: He feels stalled and undervalued at his job. That's why he's constantly angling for a raise or a promotion.

RANDALL: Maybe he just wants to get ahead.

ANDY: But he always fails. It must be very hard on him. How can he share that kind of emotion when he gets home?

ROBIN: He can't. Which brings us to his home life.

RANDALL: What's wrong with his home life? He's got a decent house, a couple of kids, a dog ...

ROBIN: And a sleeping disorder, and an eating disorder ...

RANDALL: Oh, please!

ANDY: This is a man who spends most of his time at home asleep on the couch, facing the wall.

ROBIN: And in the middle of the night, he's in the kitchen devouring everything in the refrigerator! That sound normal to you?

ANDY: Look at the women in his life. Pert, pretty and so objectified it's impossible for him to develop a real relationship with any of them ...

ROBIN: Just look at their names ...

ANDY: Blondie, Cookie, Tootsie ...

RANDALL: Okay! I admit it! Dagwood Bumstead is a typical nineties man!

(ROBIN and ANDY raise their fists and exchange a men's movement salute.)

ANDY and ROBIN: Ho!

RANDALL: *(Stands up.)* Where the hell is Stewart? *(Yells.)* Stewart!

ROBIN: Dagwood Bumstead is a man who could really benefit from the men's movement. And so could you.

RANDALL: I don't join movements, revolutions or book-of-the-month clubs.

ANDY: But how else can men come together and deal with issues like this?

ROBIN: Men need meaningful dialogue in their lives.

RANDALL: What makes you think the men's movement has cornered the market on meaningful dialogue? It's just possible that the ordinary male is not totally screwed up, you know? There are intelligent men who can carry on a reasonable conversation without a crystal.

(STEWART enters pretending a roll of toilet paper is a baseball.)

STEWART: He's going back, back, back against the wall! He's got it! The crowd goes crazy!

(The others stare at him. He starts putting the toilet paper away in his pack.)

So what were you guys talking about?

RANDALL: Nothing.

ANDY: We were talking about a comic strip, Stewart.

STEWART: Oh, yeah? Which one?

ROBIN: Dagwood.

STEWART: Dagwood? You still read Dagwood? Jeez. It's kind of fifties, don't you think? Now, Garfield is funny. I got a Garfield anthology for Christmas. *(Starts chuckling.)* Did you see the one where he sticks the dog in the waffle iron?

ANDY: Stewart?

STEWART: Yeah?

ANDY: What do you talk about when you get together with your friends? Your male friends, I mean.

STEWART: I don't get you.

ANDY: When you have a conversation. *(Beat.)* What do you talk about?

STEWART: *(Confused.)* Well ... sports, what else?

RANDALL: Okay, Andy. Point taken.

(They all leave STEWART. He scrambles to get his pack, then follows.)

STEWART: You guys see the Jays' game Saturday? The bullpen was awesome! Six K's in the last three innings.

(Music: upbeat, travelling music. The wild guys cross the stage a couple of times as the hike continues. At appropriate fade-downs in the music, we hear STEWART still talking sports while the three other guys trudge on, ignoring him.)

I saw them when they were still playing at Exhibition Stadium. Double header with the Mariners. Stieb lasted six innings ...

(They walk some more.)

I was at the game when Dave Winfield nailed that seagull ...

(Walk, walk, walk.)

Two World Series in a row! Man! I got game six of the '93 series on tape. You know, I bring it out for parties and stuff ...

(Music is replaced by the sound of a rushing river. The four wild guys wind up standing in a clump, staring disconsolately across the stage, the river in front of them. It is now early evening. The river sound stays up long enough to establish a large river and then fades to background sound.)

ROBIN: So what do we do now? Call Rescue 911?

RANDALL: I don't believe this!

ROBIN: This is the wrong valley, too, isn't it, Stewart? He's trying to get us killed, Andy.

STEWART: I'm not! Look, it's not that deep.

ROBIN: Oh, no, I'm sure! I suppose it's not cold, either.

STEWART: It's fast, but it's not that deep ...

ROBIN: *(Bitterly.)* This man tells other people what to do at work? I hope your store is well insured, Andy.

ANDY: Now, Robin ...

STEWART: *(Defensive.)* Hey, I'm a good manager! Ask anyone in Lone Pine ...

ROBIN: It was an omen. We lost our centre when we lost the crystal. We should have turned back right then.

STEWART: *(Turning to ANDY.)* ... I do special orders for customers, I give birthday cards to my staff ...

ANDY: Okay, okay, Stewart. The question is what are we going to do now? About this river.

STEWART: *(Pause.)* We cross it.

(The other guys look at him in disbelief.)

RANDALL: Why should we cross it? We'll be just as lost on the other side as we are here.

STEWART: We can't go back the way we came or we'll be up on the cliff at midnight. I say we make camp on the other side of the river. At least there's wood over there so we can build a fire.

(RANDALL tosses a twig in the river and all heads turn as it zooms away.)

ANDY: It's a pretty fast current, Stewart.

STEWART: It's not so bad. So we get our feet wet, so what?

ROBIN: So what?!

RANDALL: *(Pointing down.)* These are four-hundred-dollar leather hiking boots …

ANDY: We obviously don't have a choice. So let's stop bickering and get on with it.

(ROBIN closes his eyes and begins taking deep breaths. The others don't notice him.)

RANDALL: *(To STEWART.)* I'm sending you a bill for these boots.

ANDY: We'd better form a human chain so if one of us falls, the others can grab him before he's swept away.

ROBIN: Swept away?

(RANDALL steps into the river, grimaces at the cold and holds his arm out for the next wild guy. ROBIN is still standing off to one side. His deep breathing has become faster and he is in some danger of hyperventilating.)

RANDALL: My God, this water is freezing! Come on, let's go.

(STEWART comes next. He crosses in front of RANDALL.)

STEWART: Yaaaah, this is cold!

(STEWART links arms with RANDALL and stands in the river, a little wobbly against the current.)

RANDALL: Okay, Andy.

(ANDY steps into the river, makes his way to the end of the line, holding on to STEWART and RANDALL. ANDY slips a little as he gets to the end of the line.)

Watch it!

STEWART: *(Grabbing ANDY.)* I gotcha. Okay?

ANDY: Yeah. *(Takes his place.)* This is damn cold water!

STEWART: You're not kidding!

RANDALL: Okay, Robin. Let's go.

>   *(ROBIN is still in the same position. He opens his eyes, hesitates.)*

ROBIN: Uhhhh … You guys go ahead without me.

ANDY, RANDALL and STEWART: What?!!

RANDALL: Hurry up, Robin!

STEWART: Yeah, c'mon! We're losin' our weenies out here.

ROBIN: I can't.

RANDALL: You what?! What do you mean, you can't?!

ROBIN: I can't, that's all. I tried to visualize the crossing and I couldn't do it. I can't … go out there … in the water … I can't, that's all.

>   *(The three mid-stream wild guys look at each other, then clamber back to shore along the same chain.)*

ANDY: Robin. We just went through this with Randall. You're not in any danger.

ROBIN: I still have a latent fear of water from the time when I was six and my mother accidentally sat on me in the wading pool.

ANDY: Robin …

ROBIN: I've been working on it in therapy for the past few years.

ANDY: Robin …

ROBIN: I have this very clear image of myself struggling underwater, unable to get up. I haven't been in a swimming pool since. Whenever I think of it … *(Shudders.)*

ANDY: Robin! No one's going to sit on you in the river.

RANDALL: We promise.

ROBIN: Of course, the issue of whether it was really an accident or not has been of some concern in the sessions the last few months. What if she was playing out some deeply hidden aggression …

STEWART: Maybe she was trying to get you to shut up.

ROBIN: My therapist says I could still be harbouring resentment about that incident …

RANDALL: I'm beginning to build up a little resentment.

ANDY: What we need to do is figure out how we're going to get you across the river.

STEWART: I guess one of us could carry him …

ROBIN: Oh sure, you'll probably drop me!

ANDY: We can't carry him and keep our balance in this current. Besides, Robin needs to work this out for himself.

ROBIN: I tried the creative visualization techniques I learned at my successful life course but it didn't work.

ANDY: You're just going to have to try again.

ROBIN: The image of me standing in the river keeps being replaced by the image of my mother's ...

RANDALL: Oh, for God's sake!

ANDY: Randall, even if his fear is irrational, it's still fear and needs to be acknowledged and dealt with.

STEWART: I don't see how "visualizing" is supposed to help.

ROBIN: Well, I'm sure you wouldn't ...

STEWART: I mean he's "visualizing" himself in a river, right? Well, the guy he's visualizing is himself. And he's scared of water.

(There is a pause as they all think about this.)

Right?

ANDY: You know, maybe Stewart has a point. Maybe you should replace your image with a more positive role model.

ROBIN: Like who?

ANDY: I don't know. But what if we helped you? All of us.

ROBIN: Well, maybe. Group visualization can be very exciting ...

(STEWART and RANDALL groan.)

ANDY: *(Pointedly to RANDALL and STEWART.)* We don't want to be stuck here all night, do we? If we can help Robin to motivate himself, it's in the best interests of the entire group.

ROBIN: Andy's right.

RANDALL: *(Through clenched teeth.)* Okay, what do we have to do?

ROBIN: Well, first you sit in a circle. Preferably touching each other in some way ...

RANDALL: No touching.

STEWART: *(At the same time as RANDALL.)* Touching's out.

ANDY: Maybe you should let me lead this exercise, Robin.

ROBIN: Okay.

(They sit cross-legged in a semi-circle.)

ANDY: We need to find a common image. Someone strong and courageous, confidently stepping into the water ...

STEWART: Like ... Roy Rogers?

ANDY: Sure. Why not?

ROBIN: He had a horse. Trigger.

ANDY: Visualize him without Trigger. Imagine Roy standing beside a raging river, tough, unshakeable ...

(ROBIN straightens up and is beginning to be transformed by this vision.)

STEWART: Hey, remember in Lonesome Dove when they cross the river?

ANDY: Stewart ...

STEWART: And that guy gets into that nest of water snakes and they start wrapping themselves around him, going up his pant legs, and biting him?

ANDY: Stewart ...

STEWART: That was so cool.

ROBIN: Snakes!?

ANDY: *(To ROBIN.)* Forget about the snakes. Let's get back to Roy Rogers.

RANDALL: Jesus, Stewart.

STEWART: Hey, I'm just learning to visualize.

ANDY: Let's try it again. Okay. Roy Rogers.

STEWART, RANDALL and ROBIN: Roy Rogers.

ANDY: He's wearing a big white cowboy hat and a red bandanna around his neck ...

(STEWART and RANDALL start to hum "Happy Trails to You.")

ROBIN: I see him ...

ANDY: He strides up to the water's edge and steps in ...

ROBIN: Yeah, okay ...

ANDY: He takes one step at a time, firmly planting his boot on the river bottom, barely acknowledging the river's current ...

ROBIN: All right! I can see it!

ANDY: Now, in that mental picture you've created, substitute yourself for Roy Rogers.

(STEWART snorts.)

RANDALL: Stewart! C'mon, Robin! You're wearing your hiking shorts and rough, tough T-shirt. You step into the river …

ROBIN: Ahhh, it's cold!

ANDY: Good, good …

RANDALL: Of course it's cold! But you're Roy Rogers! You don't care! You walk all the way across. Never hesitating once …

STEWART: Hey, what if the river parts in front of him just like in The Ten Commandments?!

ANDY: Let's not get carried away, Stewart.

ROBIN: *(Stands up.)* I can see it! I can visualize it! I see me, crossing the river, fearless and brave, tough and unshakeable … Just like Roy Rogers!

(They all stand up.)

RANDALL: Okay, quick. Let's go.

(RANDALL, ANDY and STEWART start wading into the river, preparing to cross. ROBIN is still on the shore.)

ROBIN: *(Holds his arms out.)* Group hug.

RANDALL, ANDY and STEWART: What??!!

ROBIN: Group hug. Come on.

STEWART: Huh uh. No way.

ROBIN: We need to confirm that solidarity we visualized.

STEWART: No way.

ROBIN: I'm starting to lose the vision …

RANDALL: *(Menacing.)* Robin …

ANDY: Come on, you guys, it won't kill you. I'd like to get across this river sometime today.

(ANDY comes back out of the river.)

ROBIN: I'm losing it …

(RANDALL comes out of the river, too.)

RANDALL: Okay!

(ANDY, ROBIN and RANDALL group hug. STEWART hesitates, then walks out and joins the hug, an extremely uncomfortable grimace on his face. ROBIN is very pleased with himself.)

ROBIN: You see how rewarding it is to exchange real honest emotions ...?

RANDALL: *(Breaking away.)* That's enough. Let's go. Into the drink, Roy.

> *(ROBIN looks over at the river. Takes a deep breath, then strides into the river. He gasps a little from the cold, then stands, arms outstretched.)*

ROBIN: Come on, you guys! Let's move 'em out! God, I wish my analyst could see me now!!!

> *(Blackout. Suggested music: Theme song from "The Magnificent Seven." End of Act One.)*

Act Two

Scene One

(Sound: rain falling steadily on plastic. Lights up. The four wild guys crouch despondently under a tarpaulin. It is dusk. STEWART suddenly smells something. He looks down, grimaces, then takes off his hat and waves it in front of him. ROBIN gets a whiff, gives STEWART a withering look and shifts over a little closer to RANDALL. The odour travels, domino-style, down the line. All three of them look at STEWART.)

RANDALL: There's water running down the back of my neck.

ROBIN: You're not the only one who's wet, you know.

RANDALL: I don't understand what possible reason there could be for bringing a tarp that's full of holes.

STEWART: I didn't know there were holes in it.

RANDALL: It's like a huge soup strainer.

STEWART: I used it to cover my snowmobile last winter. The neighbour's kids must have been poking holes in it. Little brats.

ANDY: C'mon, you guys. Let's try to stay positive.

STEWART: Yeah. At least I thought to bring one.

ANDY: There's always something positive if you look for it.

RANDALL: A spoonful of sugar helps the medicine go down?

ANDY: I'll admit it's a simple notion …

RANDALL: At least Mary Poppins had an umbrella.

ANDY: … but it's so easy to get stuck on the idea of failure and not be able to move past it. You have to try and put the bad things behind you and just get on with it.

STEWART: You know what I could go for right now? One of those sub sandwiches we have in our Deli Delights section at the store.

RANDALL: Don't talk about food, Stewart.

STEWART: I can't help it. I'm hungry.

ROBIN: It's amazing how debilitating the male fixation on failure can be. Most of us are so success-oriented that our lives are completely out of balance.

RANDALL: And your men's group keeps you balanced?

ANDY: Not by itself, but it's a step in the right direction.

RANDALL: I don't know. Isn't it all kind of embarrassing?

ROBIN: Only when you feel threatened by it.

ANDY: There's something I wanted to try this weekend. Something we often do at our men's meeting. This might be just the time for it. I asked each of you to bring a poem ...

RANDALL: *(Groans.)* Aw, Andy ...

ANDY: ... something with personal relevance. Why don't we read them?

RANDALL: Are you sure you want to do this now?

ANDY: I can't think of a better time, Randall. It'll help keep our minds off our stomachs.

RANDALL: I don't know.

ANDY: C'mon, it's poetry. It'll raise our spirits. Tell you what, I'll go first. The poem I selected is by Rumi ...

ROBIN: Rumi! Excellent! Oh yeah!

(STEWART and RANDALL look at ROBIN's outburst of enthusiasm with incredulity.)

ANDY: Are you familiar with Rumi, Stewart?

STEWART: Well, uh ...

RANDALL: He had a roomie once. At camp.

ANDY: Rumi was a thirteenth-century Persian poet.

STEWART: Oh, yeah, right.

ROBIN: He's fantastic! We do this thing sometimes when we're drumming. We'll be in this big circle, drumming away like crazy and in the middle of the circle we'll put a book of Rumi poems. Then all of a sudden we'll stop ... like everyone will just stop for no particular reason as if we're somehow deeply in tune with each other. Anyway, someone will take the Rumi book, open it randomly and read the quatrain … *(Pauses for drama.)* on whatever page it happens to open!

RANDALL: Wow. And that's legal?

ROBIN: It's amazing how often the poem relates directly to what's in that person's psyche!

ANDY: The poem that finds you by accident is often the most revealing. Believe it or not, I opened the book randomly before I came on this weekend and this is what I found..

STEWART: Are we supposed to drum while you read?

ANDY: That won't be necessary. *(Pause, then …)*

> Keep walking, though there's no place to get to
> Don't try to see through the distances
> That's not for human beings. Move within,
> But don't move the way fear makes you move

RANDALL: Well, that was certainly …

ROBIN: A … maze … zing. Eh? Eh?

RANDALL: Am … big … u … ous.

ROBIN: If you were a little more open-minded, you might actually get something out of a poem like that.

ANDY: What about you, Stewart? Did you bring a poem?

STEWART: Well, yeah. Kind of.

ROBIN: You brought a poem?

STEWART: *(To ROBIN.)* Yes. *(Back to ANDY.)* Except, you know, when you said to bring a poem, I didn't think you meant, you know, a serious poem.

ANDY: It doesn't have to be serious, Stewart. Read it for us.

STEWART: Okay. I memorized it.
> Beans, beans, the musical fruit …

   (RANDALL starts laughing.)

ROBIN: Oh, for God's sake! He said "something with personal relevance."

STEWART: This has personal relevance.

ANDY: The idea is to celebrate the poetry of our life, not to judge it.

ROBIN: Okay. Okay. I'm sorry. You're right.

STEWART: *(Gets settled again.)*
   Beans, beans, the musical fruit
   The more you eat, the more you toot
   The more you toot, the more you fart
   The more you blow your pants apart!

RANDALL: *(Still laughing.)* Thank you for sharing that.

ROBIN: He obviously doesn't understand what poetry is.

RANDALL: Maybe you're just not open-minded enough, Robin.

ROBIN: Besides, it doesn't go like that. It's "the more you toot, the better you feel, so let's have beans for every meal."

STEWART: No way.

RANDALL: There's also "so lift your leg and let 'em squeal."

ROBIN: That's not the way it goes.

STEWART: No, no, it's "blow your pants apart." That's how my dad taught me.

ROBIN: It doesn't matter.

RANDALL: Maybe it's a cultural thing, like where you were brought up.

ROBIN: That's not how it goes …

ANDY: Robin, you brought a poem. Why don't we try yours?

ROBIN: Okay. *(Pulls out his poem.)* I brought a real poem. It was written by a man I met in Camp Medicine Mesa. I never knew his real name—I only knew him as Frog *(Composes himself.)* It's called "The Quest."

   Searching, searching
   For the path to facilitation
   For the Father's initiation
   For the wild man within
   For the pointy thrust of the horned god
   Thrusting, thrusting
   I hear the owl calling my name
   Boy-man, boy-man
   Feelings, more than feelings
   The circle of men makes fast work
   Of dysfunctional codependency
   But …

   (A pause.)

RANDALL: But … what?

ROBIN: Aha! Exactly!

STEWART: I don't get it.

RANDALL: That's because there's nothing to get.

ANDY: It's so easy to be critical, isn't it, Randall?

ROBIN: *(To RANDALL.)* I bet you didn't even bother to bring a poem, did you?

ANDY: It's much harder to venture something of your own. To open up a little and be genuine for a moment.

STEWART: At least I brought one.

RANDALL: Well, as a matter of fact, I did bring a poem.

(RANDALL pulls a piece of paper from his pocket, bows his head and breathes in deeply.)

RANDALL: When father was away on business
When lightning strikes
When the legends die
When the wind blows
When things were rotten
When time ran out
When wolves cry
When women had tails
When women lost their tails
When worlds collide
When your lover leaves
When's your birthday?
Where are the children?
Where eagles dare
Where the boys are
Where the boys are
Where the buffalo roam
Where the green ants dream
Where the red fern grows
Where the river runs black
Where's Poppa?

(There is a moment of stunned silence.)

ROBIN: Well. I have to say it. I'm impressed. You surprise me, Randall, you really do.

RANDALL: *(Modestly.)* Yes, well …

ANDY: That's an amazingly insightful poem, Randall. Where on earth did you find it?

STEWART: I think I know that poem.

ROBIN: It sums up so many things we deal with in our group. I was ... really moved. I was.

STEWART: I've read that somewhere. It's so familiar.

ROBIN: I'd like a copy of that poem. Whose is it, Bly? Snyder?

RANDALL: It's kind of obscure.

ROBIN: Creely?

STEWART: Movies! They're all movies! "Where Eagles Dare," Clint Eastwood and Richard Burton. "Where the Boys Are," Connie Francis and Yvette Mimieux. "Where the Buffalo Roam," Bill Murray.

ROBIN: What are you talking about?

STEWART: They're movies, man! Every line in the poem is a movie title.

ANDY: Is that true, Randall?

STEWART: It wasn't really a poem.

ROBIN: They're movies?!

RANDALL: Okay. I couldn't find any poetry books at home. I tore a page out of the index of my Home Video Companion.

STEWART: *(To ANDY.)* At least I brought a real poem.

ANDY: You may think that you read a nonsensical list of movie titles, but wasn't it interesting how personally relevant many of those lines were to your own life, Randall?

RANDALL: It's a random page torn out of a movie index, Andy.

ANDY: And yet it contained references to your father, your childhood ...

ROBIN: You think you tore the page out at random, but really the page found you. It's your inner child crying out through your subconscious. "Where's Poppa?" How much more direct can that be?

RANDALL: *(Standing up.)* Hey, you know what? I think it's quit raining.

STEWART: All right! About time!

(STEWART and ROBIN start to fold up the plastic tarpaulin.)

ANDY: What's important about poetry is how it touches our lives.

RANDALL: My "poem," as you call it, is no more meaningful or personally relevant than Stewart's.

ROBIN: Oh, no?

RANDALL: No. My poem was a joke, that's all. Not unlike the idea of Stewart guiding this hike.

STEWART: *(To ANDY.)* He's jealous 'cause he's the only one who didn't bring a real poem. But that's okay. I understand. A good manager needs to stay focused on the positive aspects of every situation.

RANDALL: Oh, please.

ROBIN: You know what your problem is, Randall?

RANDALL: Yes. I'm wet and hungry.

ROBIN: You close yourself off to the creative forces at work in the universe. You'll never have a truly creative experience because you've got all these barriers up.

RANDALL: Jesus! Robin, would you just …

ANDY: All right, you guys, that's enough! Look, we're all tired and wet and hungry. Let's do something about it. We've probably got an hour's worth of light left. Let's fan out and see if we can find something to eat.

RANDALL: What are we looking for? Free-range chickens?

ANDY: We can look for berries, edible shoots … Robin, you must have had some idea of what we were going to do for food.

ROBIN: Yeah! Absolutely!

ANDY: All right. Well then, let's go!

STEWART: *(Listening.)* Did you hear that?

RANDALL: What?

(They all listen.)

ROBIN: It was the wind.

STEWART: Didn't sound like the wind to me.

RANDALL: What if it's a bear?

ANDY: It's not a bear. Come on.

STEWART: But it might be a bear.

RANDALL: Remember that anthill we passed?

ANDY: Any number of creatures could have done that, Randall.

RANDALL: Whatever it was, it was big. And had big claws.

STEWART: Like a bear.

ANDY: Bears don't come into this terrain at this time of year. So there's nothing to worry about.

ROBIN: It's not a bear. Andy knows about bears and he says it's not a bear. So, it's not a bear.

ANDY: Right. Okay. Let's go.

ROBIN: Right.

RANDALL: Okay.

ANDY: You coming, Stewart?

STEWART: Out there? Uh ... you go ahead. I'll look for food around here.

(They all leave STEWART by himself. He looks around for a moment, then ...)

(Leaps up.) Hey, you guys, wait up!

(Blackout. Suggested music: Drums.)

Scene Two

(Lights up. STEWART, RANDALL and ANDY sit around a small campfire. Four sleeping bags are stretched out around them. ANDY holds a Tilley Endurables hat, full of berries. Music fades.)

RANDALL: It's just I thought the idea was we would pool the berries we picked and then divide them up.

ANDY: And that's just what we're doing ...

RANDALL: Yeah, except Stewart was standing right beside me grazing in the bushes like a bull moose.

STEWART: I was not.

RANDALL: Yes, you were. I saw you. Do you do that in your produce section at work? I don't see why we should have to share the berries we picked while he was filling his face.

STEWART: I wasn't filling my face.

ANDY: Okay. I make out eighty-three saskatoon berries here. It's not great, but it's the best we could do given the light. So that's twenty berries each.

(ANDY counts out his berries, then passes the hat to STEWART who begins counting out his berries.)

RANDALL: Plus one extra for everyone except Stewart.

STEWART: *(Dumps his berries back in the hat and hands it to RANDALL.)* Here. They're all yours. Cry-baby.

ANDY: Don't you think this is getting just a little petty? Look, we've climbed a mountain and crossed a river today. Our feet hurt—I know mine do—and we're all a little tired …

(Enter ROBIN. He has a bandanna tied around his head, something like blood smeared on his cheeks, and he carries a stick which he imagines is a spear. He walks energetically toward the campfire, hopping on one foot then the other, ready to dance around it.)

RANDALL: What are you doing?

ROBIN: A warrior should celebrate his fire. Yeah! Celebrate the evening feast! Come on, you guys!

STEWART: What've you got all over your face?

ROBIN: The blood of the prey!

RANDALL: Saskatoon berries?

ROBIN: Well, we haven't caught any prey yet. But that's what the books say you're supposed to do … Hey, I know, we could build a sweat lodge!

ANDY: Why don't you just sit down and eat your supper, Robin?

RANDALL: Someone forgot to bring their Quaaludes.

ROBIN: What kind of warriors are you guys, anyway? We should be celebrating our accomplishments. But you guys don't want to do anything.

RANDALL: You mean other than eat and sleep indoors?

ROBIN: Hey, I lost a very important object today … *(The others all groan.)* A sacred object … but I'm getting through it. I'm ready to keep the spirit of the weekend alive. Which is more than I can say for you guys.

ANDY: Robin's right. Granted, a few things haven't gone the way we expected. But we can still accomplish what we came here for.

ROBIN: Yeah! When I was at Mendocino, we built a fifteen-foot wooden penis and did a very emotional naming ceremony around it.

RANDALL: Let me guess. You named it Dick.

ROBIN: No. We named each other. But obviously, you guys aren't ready for that kind of breakthrough.

RANDALL: I'm definitely not.

ROBIN: I'm trying to pass on the benefit of my experience, in the tradition of male oral culture.

STEWART: Who wants another beer?

(They all accept a beer this time, even ROBIN.)

ROBIN: While you guys were arguing over a handful of saskatoon berries, I was setting a rabbit snare. In the morning, we'll be roasting rabbit over our breakfast fire.

RANDALL: Where did you learn to set a rabbit snare? The New York Times Guide to Outdoor Gastronomy?

ROBIN: The Weekend Warrior Handbook, New Age edition.

RANDALL: I hope you won't be offended if I don't start sautéing the onions yet. Anyway, bunny breakfast or not, I think we should just forget about looking for this cabin and concentrate on finding our way back tomorrow.

STEWART: Go back?

ROBIN: Oh, I see. You're just going to give up.

RANDALL: I'm not giving up. We're lost. I think it would be prudent to make an effort to get home.

ROBIN: Good thing you didn't go on that triathlon with your girlfriend. It's not a sport for quitters.

STEWART: We could still find the lake tomorrow.

RANDALL: How many more valleys are we going to try, Stewart?

ROBIN: When the going gets tough, the tough run for their BMW's.

RANDALL: Robin …

ANDY: The real-life challenges we're facing do present us with a unique opportunity. A man's true character emerges under pressure. The pampered lives we lead in the city never give us the opportunity to explore that aspect of ourselves. I mean, who are we, really?

RANDALL: The four stooges.

ANDY: Now that we've been challenged in a physical way, are we courageous enough, Randall, to look farther and challenge ourselves emotionally?

RANDALL: I'm sorry, Andy, but all this navel-gazing gives me the willies.

ROBIN: You're afraid of what you might find.

RANDALL: Lint, that's all. Look, I feel sufficiently challenged for one day. My warrior instincts are telling me to go home and order a pizza.

STEWART: Well, I think Andy's right. Okay, so I got us lost. We can still make the best of it. We can still turn this into a successful weekend. Just like I did with Hawaiian Krazy Daze. You remember my Hawaiian Krazy Daze promotion, right, Andy?

ANDY: Oh, yes. I remember.

STEWART: Palm trees made outa crepe paper? The checkout girls in hula skirts? That was all my idea. And talk about moving produce. Hey, we sold one heck of a lotta pineapples.

ANDY: Which was fortunate since you ordered an entire truckload by mistake.

STEWART: Yeah, okay, but we sold most of 'em, right? I mean, it could have been worse. I really think that shows I'm ready for more responsibility.

RANDALL: Just be sure he has a map when he sets out for the frozen foods, Andy.

STEWART: *(Ignoring RANDALL.)* You see, the thing is, I've been managing the store in Lone Pine for ten years now. I feel like I'm ready for a new challenge within the organization. A bigger store maybe.

ANDY: Hawaiian Krazy Daze certainly showed what you're capable of.

STEWART: Thinking on your feet. Adapting to new challenges. That's what it takes to be a good manager, right, Andy?

ANDY: Let's talk business another time, Stewart.

STEWART: Another time. *(Dawning on him that it might be positive.)* Another time! Okay! All right! Then let's have some fun! I mean we're on a guys' weekend, right? We still have some beer. It's quit raining. The old lady isn't here to tell us to mow the lawn or clean up dog pooh. We're free! Whoooo!!

ROBIN: Whooo!!!

STEWART: Hey, Rob, you brought your guitar. Why don't you give us a tune?

(STEWART grabs the guitar and hands it to ROBIN.)

ROBIN: *(Fake modesty.)* Well ... I don't know ...

STEWART: I know most of the chords to a few Neil Young songs ...

ROBIN: *(Quickly grabs the guitar from STEWART.)* There is one piece I've been working on.

STEWART: Right on! Okay, what is it? Dylan?

ROBIN: Actually, it's my own composition.

STEWART: Wow. Great.

ROBIN: I was at Mendocino in May for a combined Encountering Your Inner Shadow and Power Dancing workshop. I was meditating by myself one day when I started watching this bumblebee as it was approaching a flower. It was a beautiful dance of power and yielding. So I wrote this piece. It's called ... "Encounter."

(ROBIN pauses dramatically, then in an overblown way, plinks the strings of the guitar above the bridge. He pauses again, then attacks the bass string, thumping up and down on the same three notes in imitation of a four-hundred-pound bumblebee. Pause. Plink. Thump. ROBIN ends his song with a flourish. There is a long empty pause.)

STEWART: Do you know any Creedence?

RANDALL: That's the stupidest thing I've ever heard.

ANDY: That was very interesting, Robin. You know, Robert Bly says that the whole men's movement is about dancing with grief. I felt an echo of that sentiment in your song.

RANDALL: The question is, whose grief is it? His or the audience's?

STEWART: What about Beach Boys? Do you do any Beach Boys?

ROBIN: It's the dual grief of the bee and the flower. And Andy's right. Grief is the cornerstone of the men's movement.

RANDALL: You mean self-indulgence is the cornerstone of the men's movement.

STEWART: Okay. Maybe a tune wasn't the right idea. Why don't we try some of that breathing thing, that in-out thing, you know, centre-of-the-earth, top-of-the-head stuff?

ROBIN: I'd suggest we try a naming ceremony but we don't have a crystal.

STEWART: We don't need to have the crystal, do we? *(Hands him a rock lying on the ground.)* How about if we use this?

ROBIN: We can't just use any old rock. It has to be a conductor, a spiritual vessel …

STEWART: *(Holds out his beer bottle.)* Well, how about this? It's kinda like crystal.

ROBIN: You want to imbue a beer bottle with psychic energy?

RANDALL: Aw come on, Rob. It's just a symbol after all.

STEWART: It's sorta the same colour as your crystal. *(Holds it up.)* Sometimes you can see things in it … Oh …

(STEWART sees there's some beer left in the bottle and finishes it off.)

ROBIN: Oh good, we're going to have a psychedelic experience with a beer bottle.

ANDY: Well, what do you think, Robin? Do you want to try a naming ceremony with the beer bottle as a substitute crystal?

STEWART: *(Hands ROBIN the beer bottle.)* Yeah, gwan, take a whack at it.

ROBIN: I dunno, Andy. I feel there's a sort of psychic vacuum around this campfire.

ANDY: You have to remember that you've had a great deal more experience in this area than Randall or Stewart. You'd expect a little scepticism, wouldn't you?

ROBIN: I suppose.

ANDY: Neither of them knew much about visualization, but we tried it and it was very successful, wasn't it?

ROBIN: That's true.

RANDALL: Sure. You're the expert in all this, we're the stupid Philistines. So tell us, what's a naming ceremony?

ROBIN: A naming ceremony is designed to discover a man's true name. The name he carries deep in his soul, the one that best expresses his inner self.

RANDALL: What's yours? Rhumbas with Rabbits?

ROBIN: Oh, that's it! That's enough. We'll just forget about having a meaningful men's weekend. You've been harassing and ridiculing us every time we've tried to do anything of real value. So if that's the way you want it, let's just sit out here and stick with our blind, male behaviour patterns.

STEWART: Ah, Robin. Don't be upset. Come on, what was your name?

ROBIN: I'm not telling.

ANDY: Why don't you tell them, Robin. They won't laugh.

ROBIN: Yes, they will.

RANDALL: No, we promise. Scout's honour.

ROBIN: I don't believe you.

STEWART: No, really. Tell us.

ROBIN: No! My other name is very special and I'm not going to just lay it out for you guys to ridicule. Absolutely not! I will not tell you!

(A long pause.)

STEWART: Well, hey, I could play a song …

ROBIN: *(Grabs the empty beer bottle and holds it up.)* Ra Ho Tep.

(RANDALL and STEWART struggle to contain their laughter.)

See? I knew it.

RANDALL: Ra Ho Tep??

ANDY: Now, we promised.

ROBIN: I discovered about two years ago at a Past Life Regression Workshop that I used to be an Egyptian holy man in about 430 B.C.

RANDALL: Oh my God, we've got a sick puppy here.

ROBIN: *(Holds up the beer bottle.)* I believe I have the floor.

RANDALL: Sorry.

ROBIN: I'm telling you, this is the real thing. The workshop was led by Jay Zee Knight. *(Dramatic pause, waits for reaction but doesn't get it.)* You know, the medium who channelled for Shirley MacLaine?

STEWART and RANDALL: Ohhhhh …

ROBIN: I was keeper of the sacred temple of Osiris near Luxor. *(Pause, leans forward, dramatic.)* But I was murdered …

RANDALL: I can believe that.

ROBIN: For political reasons. I won't get into the details because you wouldn't understand but suffice it to say that my quest for spiritual enlightenment goes back many lifetimes. I am what they call "a seeker." And the seeker is always mocked and misunderstood. Especially by those whose only goal in life is to sleep with an entire sorority.

RANDALL: Are you finished?

ROBIN: Yes.

(ROBIN sets the beer bottle down. RANDALL reaches over, grabs the beer bottle and holds it up to show he has the floor.)

RANDALL: Okay. I've been listening to you go on and on about how enlightened you are and how you've got all the answers for the modern man. Well, if you've got it all figured out, how come you feel the need to go to every New Age mumbo-jumbo workshop that comes along? I mean, get a life, Robin. Your own life.

ROBIN: That just shows how much you know about …

RANDALL: *(Holds up beer bottle.)* Uh, uh … my turn. Group visualization, your buddy Frog the poet, a fifteen-foot wooden penis. Now you're onto past life regression and Shirley MacLaine's channeller, for God's sake! This stuff is all interchangeable to you, isn't it?

STEWART: *(Takes the last swallow of beer from his beer bottle and holds it up.)* You wanna know what I think?

ROBIN and RANDALL: No.

ROBIN: It's a cumulative process, Randall …

RANDALL: *(Waves the beer bottle at him.)* Uh, uh … I think you're so desperately bored with yourself that you'd buy into any half-witted, self-help con game that's going. Let's just do a little survey here. You can answer by nodding your head for "yes" or shaking it for "no." Have you ever had dinner with the Hari Krishna?

(ROBIN hesitates, then nods.)

Have you ever taken a Scientology personality test?

(ROBIN nods again.)

Are your best friends therapists?

(ROBIN nods again, with a hang-dog look.)

Have you ever been Rolfed? Did you participate in the cosmic convergence? Have you ever had a colonic? Do you own a Ravi Shankar record?

(ROBIN lunges at RANDALL and tries to grab the beer bottle away as RANDALL continues, holding the bottle just out of range.)

Have you ever been on an EST weekend? Do you own a tape with only the sounds of falling rain on it? Are you now or have you ever been an Amway distributor?

(ROBIN grabs another beer bottle and holds it up.)

ROBIN: There have to be seekers willing to take chances! Yes, and willing to make mistakes, if necessary. For the sake of the planet!

RANDALL: Don't forget the baby seals.

ROBIN: We have to re-invent what it means to be a man! And we have to do it quickly, before the planet is destroyed!

RANDALL: You don't give a shit about the planet. You're so self-absorbed there's no room in your psyche for anyone but you. All of you. Ra Ho Tep, Shirley MacLaine, Bunny Stalker ... When was the last time you had something in your life that wasn't about you, that wasn't about breathing through your anus or analysing your poor long-suffering father ...

ROBIN: Leave my father out of it.

RANDALL: All that shit about mythopoetic heritage! Your father probably can't stand to be around you. Just like everyone else.

(ROBIN stops. RANDALL, too, stops, realizing he's gone too far. A pause. Then ROBIN bursts into tears.)

ROBIN: *(Through the sobs.)* My father died when I was ten years old. *(Continues to sob relentlessly.)*

(The other three men are initially paralysed by his weeping and don't know what to do.)

STEWART: *(Embarrassed by the crying.)* Aww, Jesus, Rob ...

ANDY: That's okay, Robin, let it go ...

RANDALL: Wait a second! This isn't fair! This is how women get out of arguments!

ROBIN: *(Continues sobbing.)* I can't help it.

STEWART: Yeah, c'mon, Rob. Stop crying.

ROBIN: You're supposed to cry over your father on weekends like this! I loved my dad.

(RANDALL takes a deep breath and goes over to ROBIN. He sits beside him as ROBIN continues to sob.)

RANDALL: *(Sympathetic.)* It's okay. You should be able to cry if you want.

ROBIN: It's not like I try to be an asshole, you know? I know I'm self-absorbed. Don't you think I know that? I'm thirty-eight and I've lived alone all my adult life. I watched my mother grow old alone. I'm scared it'll happen to me.

RANDALL: I know how you feel.

ROBIN: Oh, sure. How would you know?

RANDALL: My dad died when I was fifteen.

(ROBIN looks up, a little incredulously, at RANDALL.)

ROBIN: He did?

RANDALL: Heart attack. Runs in our family. *(Beat.)* I loved my dad, too.

(ROBIN and RANDALL look at each other: a moment of recognition. STEWART picks up the guitar and starts to strum Neil Young's "Heart of Gold.")

STEWART: I wanna live … I wanna give … I've been a miner for a heart of gold …

STEWART and RANDALL: It's these expressions … I never give …

(Everyone joins in. It's a soulful rendition, with each of them manfully trying to hit the high notes, just like Neil.)

ALL: That keep me searchin' for a heart of gold … and I'm gettin' old … keep me searchin' for a heart of gold and I'm gettin' old …

(Blackout. Music: their singing cross-fades into Neil Young's version of "Heart of Gold.")

Scene Three

(Music fades. Lights up on the four sleeping wild guys. They are all tucked into their sleeping bags around the smouldering fire. It is the dead of night now and the stars twinkle overhead. There is a rustling sound in the bushes, off.)

STEWART: *(Sits up.)* What was that?

(The others sit up groggily.)

RANDALL: Huh?

STEWART: I heard something in the bushes.

ANDY: Is something out there?

STEWART: Shhh. Listen.

ROBIN: *(Getting up excited.)* It's a rabbit! I caught a rabbit in the snare! All right!

(ROBIN hesitates.)

RANDALL: Well, you better go and get it.

ROBIN: I could get it in the morning.

RANDALL: It might be suffering.

STEWART: Yeah, you better go and ... you know ... finish it off.

ROBIN: *(To STEWART.)* Do you wanna go? You're sort of a northern guy.

STEWART: Sorry. I work in produce.

ANDY: You better go and check it out, Robin.

RANDALL: I hate to think of that poor little bunny, garrotted in the moonlight. Thrashing his little cottontail back and forth ... Remember in the Godfather when Luka Brazzi ...

ROBIN: Okay. Okay, I'm going!

(ROBIN exits reluctantly.)

STEWART: We're not gonna put bunny blood on our faces, are we?

ANDY: No.

RANDALL: Where did you meet Robin, anyway?

ANDY: He showed up at our men's group one night. I think he was just lonely. I know he's a little hard to take at times, but I like him. I like his sincerity.

ROBIN: *(Off.)* Oh my God!!!

(ROBIN enters running.)

That's no bunny out there!

RANDALL: You're no bunny till some bunny loves you.

ROBIN: *It's a bear!!*

(They all leap up in a panic.)

STEWART: Oh jeez! I hate bears!

ROBIN: *(Searching in a panic.)* Where's my spear? Where's my spear?

STEWART: I hate bears! I really hate bears!

ANDY: Are you sure it was a bear?

ROBIN: Oh, yeah, it's a bear! It's big, it's really big! And it's right out there!

STEWART: It's probably a grizzly!

ROBIN: A grizzly!?! Why didn't you tell us we were in grizzly country?!?

STEWART: I didn't know, okay?

ANDY: I suppose it could be a bear.

ROBIN: *It's a bear!!*

STEWART: I really hate bears … I really hate bears … I really hate bears …

RANDALL: No one said anything about us being breakfast.

STEWART: I really hate bears … I really hate bears …

ANDY: Now, calm down, all of you. It's most likely just a common black bear. They're nocturnal feeders … he's probably looking for berries or an ant hill …

RANDALL: Or a late-night lawyer snack.

ANDY: *(Putting sticks on the fire.)* We'll build up the fire and he'll move on … no trouble …

(The rustling sound in the bushes is coming closer.)

STEWART: He's coming closer!!!

ROBIN, STEWART and RANDALL: Yaaa!!!

(Blackout. Suggested music: Something spooky, with slide guitar and drums.)

Scene Four

(Lights up on the four wild guys, sitting nervously around the campfire. No one has been able to go back to sleep. Now they all hold sticks, sharpened into spears. Music fades.)

RANDALL: I feel like I'm at a weenie roast.

ROBIN: They're spears. Think of them as spears.

RANDALL: All right. A Cro-Magnon weenie roast.

ROBIN: Spears are better than nothing.

RANDALL: Oh sure. How would you know? This is the guy who was trying to get out of offing the bunny.

STEWART: I hate bears, you know? I really hate bears.

ANDY: There's nothing to worry about. With all the noise you guys made, that bear is probably five miles from here right now.

RANDALL: I don't see you giving up your spear.

ROBIN: You know, this is kind of a "primal moment."

RANDALL: And I didn't bring a camera.

ROBIN: I mean, here we are, a group of men, hunters, huddled around our fire for protection while wild beasts prowl in the darkness.

STEWART: A bear went right past our tent once when my wife and I were camping at Sylvan Lake. Maxie was scared out of her mind. God! I really hate that!

ANDY: Actually, Robin's right. Most remnants of our instinctual behaviour go back to times when we dwelt in caves and had to compete for shelter with bears. This is a very archetypal situation.

STEWART: *(Tapping his stick on the ground.)* I don't even like camping, you know? You live up north and people expect you to be like Grizzly Adams—build your own log cabin, trap your own clothing. I mean, jeez, I live for my VCR like everybody else.

(The guys have started to pay attention to STEWART.)

ANDY: You know, bears are principally vegetarian. Even if the bear were still around here, which it's not, there's no way it would attack four men around a fire, Stewart.

STEWART: Unless it's a grizzly. They're crazy. They hunt people.

ANDY: I'm sure it's just a black bear.

STEWART: Yeah? Well, what if it's a black bear with rabies? You never know, eh? Maxie just freaks out if she thinks there's bears around.

ROBIN: Not like you.

STEWART: No, I'm not scared of bears. I just hate 'em.

RANDALL: *(Pause. He starts tapping his stick like STEWART.)* Me too. I'm not scared of 'em. I just hate 'em.

(STEWART looks over at RANDALL. There's a pause.)

What about you, Robin? Are you scared of bears?

ROBIN: You're damn right I'm scared of bears. Are you kidding? Do you realize that …

(RANDALL whacks ROBIN in the knee with his stick, then keeps tapping.)

Ow!

(ROBIN looks at RANDALL, then smiles, starts to tap his stick.)

No, I'm not scared of bears. I hate 'em.

(The three guys grin at each other and start tapping their sticks louder.)

RANDALL: Yeah. We aren't scared of bears. But we sure hate 'em!
STEWART: *(Grinning.)* Yeah!
   (RANDALL starts a chant that ROBIN and STEWART join in on.)
RANDALL, STEWART and ROBIN: We aren't scared of bears, but we sure hate 'em! We aren't scared of bears, but we sure hate 'em! We aren't scared of bears, but we sure hate 'em!
RANDALL: What about you, Andy? You hate bears, too, right?
ANDY: No. I really like bears. And I'm not afraid of them, either. I respect them, but I'm not afraid of them.
   (They all stop tapping their sticks.)
RANDALL: Jesus.
ANDY: But I liked what you were doing just now. Acknowledging the fear you have in common by denying it in a ritualistic way. Keep going if you want.
ROBIN: Somehow we've lost the spontaneity of the moment.
ANDY: Men have been taught to suppress fear. It's equated with courage in our culture but nothing could be farther from the truth. For modern men, the expression of their deepest inner fears may be the single most courageous act of their lives.
RANDALL: So you're not scared of bears. But you're scared of something, right?
ANDY: Everyone's afraid of something.
RANDALL: So? What is it for you?
   (ANDY doesn't answer.)
ROBIN: Well, I'm afraid of women.
RANDALL: Did your analyst tell you that?
ROBIN: Well, yeah. But it's true. I don't know how to behave with them.
RANDALL: It's just a matter of self-confidence. Women want you to act like you know what you're doing. Even if you don't.
ROBIN: I get so confused. I can't seem to keep a relationship going. The last time, it was this woman, Lorraine. She's a regular customer down at the Eco-Store. Every time she came in we'd have these great conversations over the crushed glass bin. But it still took me a year and a half to work up the courage to ask her out. We go to this cappuccino bar and I'm so nervous, I knock back three double *lattes* and I'm, like, hovering six inches above the stool. After awhile, she

gets this glazed look in her eyes. Hasn't returned one of my calls since. I don't know. Maybe I try too hard. *(To RANDALL.)* I guess you don't have that kind of problem.

RANDALL: *(Pause.)* I used to be married.

ANDY: I didn't know that.

RANDALL: Yeah. For seven years.

(A pause.)

ROBIN: And ...?

RANDALL: It didn't work out.

ROBIN: What happened?

RANDALL: I was fast-tracking. Making good money, staying out a lot after work. You get so you think you're invincible, that the world is there for your own personal benefit. You think you'll never have to regret anything you do. *(Pause.)* Twenty-five-year-old para-legal. After awhile, the guilt started to get to me. I couldn't take it, you know? I broke it off and told my wife what had been going on. *(Shakes his head.)* She didn't care. We'd let things get so bad, you know, it just didn't matter to her. So we split up. Nothing's been right ever since. I can't seem to get back on my feet.

STEWART: When I was just out of high school, I got a date with that year's Miss Lone Pine. It was a big deal, you know—I borrowed a friend's pick-up and everything. I went to kiss her and wound up accidentally elbowing her in the nose. She starts bleeding all over the cab so I go to hand her some kleenex, right, and my ID bracelet gets caught and rips her dress. She freaks out, like she thinks I'm attacking her. I wasn't! I mean, I'm not that kind of guy!

ROBIN: What'd you do?

STEWART: Well, you know, I took her home. Spent the rest of the night trying to get the blood out of the shag carpeting on my friend's dashboard.

RANDALL: And the whole town found out about it, right?

STEWART: She never told anybody. Neither did I. But I always felt so ... guilty about it, you know? I mean, it was an accident. I'm kinda ... *(Looks over at ANDY.)* I used to be kinda ... clumsy. That's all.

RANDALL: No one ever explains this stuff. You're just supposed to know how to behave with women.

ROBIN: Yeah, like someone goes presto ... you're Prince Charles.

RANDALL: Prince Charles?

(ROBIN shrugs and then grins a little sheepishly.)

STEWART: Anyway, that's the great thing about my wife, Maxie, eh? I don't have to put on a bunch of phoney stuff for her. She loves me for what I am, you know? Even if I mess up sometimes.

ROBIN: Women are the most frustrating, indecipherable, completely unfathomable mystery! All the women I've ever gone out with wanted me to be someone else.

RANDALL: *(Teasing.)* And you were.

(ROBIN gives RANDALL a dirty look. Then they both smile.)

STEWART: This is sorta cool, you know? I never talk about stuff like this with the guys on the ballteam.

ROBIN: Well, maybe you should.

STEWART: *(Laughs.)* Are you outta your mind? *(Thinks of an example.)* This guy, Steve? We play ball together twice a week, right? His wife left him two months ago. I find out the day before yesterday! Man!

ANDY: The break-up of a relationship can be one of the hardest things to talk about.

STEWART: But like we're buddies, right? Why wouldn't he tell me?

ANDY: Dr. Rothenberg says the natural impulse is to protect the wound from your own social circle. It's often falsely perceived as a personal failure, a betrayal of society's social contract. There's a lot of guilt attached …

RANDALL: *(Finally tired of all this.)* Andy. We're talking about Stewart's friend here and you're talking psychosocial theory.

ANDY: We need to be able to step back and learn as we go along. In the same way that Tai Chi teaches you to absorb your opponent's energy and rechannel it.

RANDALL: Well, that's great for Buddhist monks. But what about Steve? We're talking about a real person here.

ANDY: I was just trying to make the point that guilt is a very strong emotion.

ROBIN: No kidding. I feel guilty all the time. Especially with women. Starting with my mother. She made me feel guilty for everything. Even the fact that my father wasn't around anymore.

RANDALL: That wasn't your fault.

ROBIN: I know, but the guilt is still there. I feel guilty when I hear the newest violence against women statistics. I feel guilty about sexism on MTV. I feel guilty about inequality in the workplace ...

RANDALL: The hole in the ozone ...

ROBIN: Yeah, that one's my fault, too. Laundry detergent commercials. The slave trade of the 17th century, the industrial revolution, leg hold traps ...

RANDALL: Willie and Julio ...

STEWART: I feel guilty about leaving the toilet seat up ...

ROBIN: All the unresolved North American Native land claims, the automobile, PCBs ...

STEWART: PMS.

RANDALL: Not getting pregnant.

ROBIN: The pill, breast implants, high-heeled shoes ...

RANDALL: Paul Anka.

ROBIN: I feel like I've absorbed responsibility for every rotten thing that's ever happened on the planet just because I have a penis. So, I have all these wonderful deeply empathetic talks with women about how men have screwed up the world and ...

RANDALL: *(At the same time as ROBIN.)* They all think you're a wimp.

ROBIN: They all think I'm a wimp. So I go out on a few of these men's retreats to try and discover what being a modern, responsible man is about and now they're calling me ...

RANDALL: Anti-feminist.

ROBIN: Anti-feminist. *(Stands.)* Well, I'm sorry but I read Doris Lessing novels. I go to the feminist film festivals. I would never personally pay a woman less than a man for the same job. I don't tell sexist jokes. I know there's a lot of bad asses out there but *(Cries out to the heavens.) I'm not one of them!!*

RANDALL and STEWART: Yeah!!

ANDY: It doesn't have to be so confrontational. Barbara and I have found a balance that works for us.

RANDALL: Oh, Maharishi, please tell us what it is ...

ANDY: She has an absorbing and fulfilling career. I have an absorbing and fulfilling career.

RANDALL: And you meet in Moose Jaw every six months.

ANDY: It's true that we don't see each other as much as we'd like to but, it's part of being intellectually active and living a full life.

RANDALL: Intellectually active is kind of an understatement, don't you think?

ANDY: What do you mean?

RANDALL: The last twenty-four hours have been like you're the twelve-year-old and we're the ant farm. I mean, this group isn't totally equal, is it? We're not exactly the four musketeers. All for one and one for all.

ROBIN: Yeah, Randall's right. We're hanging out all over the place here and you're making notes. I've known you for two years and I didn't know you had a wife. You've never talked about her.

ANDY: Well, I do have a wife. *(Pause.)* I have a teenage son as well.

RANDALL: You have a son? So, you're the absent father that Bly talks about. How come you didn't bring your son?

ANDY: He couldn't come.

RANDALL: Why not? What about quality time? How come you brought us out here and left your own kid at home?

ANDY: I couldn't bring Danny.

STEWART: Why not?

ANDY: *(With difficulty.)* He's on probation. He's not allowed out of the city.

(The guys are all a little shocked. They pause.)

STEWART: What did he do?

ANDY: *(Pause.)* He vandalized a graveyard. A Jewish graveyard. I don't know why. A year in therapy later and still I don't know why. Where does that come from? Me? In some way I can't understand?

STEWART: My brother stole a car when he was sixteen and got busted, but he turned out to be a good guy. Who knows why young guys do some of the things they do, eh? Mom and Dad stuck with him and he was okay, you know?

(ANDY walks to the far edge of the stage and turns his back to the others.)

ANDY: Did you know that in many primitive tribes, boys are kidnapped by the men of the village at a certain age to symbolize their passage from the world of women to the world of men? Often a physical wound is inflicted to be a constant reminder that the boy is now initiated.

ROBIN: Andy. Come and sit by the fire with us.

ANDY: *(With his back still to the group.)* The idea of male initiation is embedded in the collective unconscious …

RANDALL: Andy? Don't bullshit us, okay? If you don't want to talk to us, that's all right. But don't bullshit us.

ROBIN: Come back to the fire.

(ANDY pauses, then comes back to the fire and sits down.)

RANDALL: It's not a sin to talk about yourself, Andy.

STEWART: Look, you set up this whole weekend so we could get in touch with our feelings. But, like, you're the only one not doin' it. How come?

ANDY: I don't think I know how.

RANDALL: *(Gently.)* I think you do.

(The other guys wait.)

ANDY: *(Takes a deep breath.)* This thing with Danny, it's ruined our marriage. Or our marriage ruined Danny. I don't know which. *(Pause.)* Barbara's having an affair.

STEWART: Oh, man.

ANDY: She doesn't know that I know. But I do. I don't blame her, really. I understand that she needed someone, I just … She's probably with him right now, at this very moment. *(Struggling.)* There's something … *(Hand to his chest.)* … in here. I don't know what. Something brooding, dangerous … I feel like everything I've done all these years … that it's all been for nothing … or worse, much worse.

RANDALL: You're pissed off, Andy. Admit it.

ANDY: All right! Yes! I am pissed off! I am … outraged! My little … my son is embracing everything I despise in this world. I have this … urge, this overwhelming urge, to break his rotten neck! And my wife … she's abandoned us both, exactly when we needed her most! How could she do such a thing!

(ANDY grips the spear so fiercely that he may indeed lash out, at anything. Suddenly, the rage seems to pass.)

(Quietly.) No. *(He throws down the spear.)* No.

ROBIN: But, you need to let your anger go …

ANDY: No. What I need is time to think. I need to ... start again somehow. I'm fifty years old and I still don't understand anything. *(Beat.)* I feel so ... lost.

(RANDALL reaches out and embraces ANDY in a hug. ROBIN joins the hug, then STEWART.)

RANDALL: Guess what, brother? We're all hopelessly fucking lost. And we always have been. *(Pause.)* But there is one great satisfaction in all this.

ROBIN: What?

RANDALL: At least we know ... *(Points at STEWART.)* It's all his fault!!

(STEWART is taken aback at first. But RANDALL starts to smile. ANDY and ROBIN start to laugh. Soon they're all laughing hysterically. Suddenly, ROBIN stops cold and looks off stage.)

ROBIN: Oh, my God! Nobody move!

(The guys all freeze and look where ROBIN's looking.)

(Points.) He's right there.

(There is a loud rustling in the bushes and the snuffling and grunting of a bear, off. The guys back away from the sound so they end up in a frightened clump.)

RANDALL: Oh, shit!

STEWART: Jesus!

RANDALL: Oh, shit, oh, shit ...

ROBIN: Andeee ... What do we do now?

(ANDY stands and picks up a spear.)

ANDY: *(Toward the bear, quietly, but firmly.)* Go bruin go!

(The other three guys just look at him.)

(A little louder.) Go bruin go! Go bruin go!

STEWART: Look! He's leaving.

(The others jump up and join in the chant, shaking their spears. RANDALL picks up the drum and begins to beat it in time.)

ALL: Go bruins go! Go bruins go! Go bruins go!!!

(They all start leaping around the fire to the beat of the drum, screaming at the top of their lungs and laughing foolishly at each other.)

ALL: *(Hockey chant.)* Let's go, bruins, let's go! Let's go, bruins, let's go! Let's go, bruins, let's go!

(Blackout. Suggested music: "Brother Blood" by the Neville Brothers.)

Scene Five

(Lights up. Music fades. It's morning. The wild guys, minus ANDY, are lying in their sleeping bags. STEWART wakes up first.)

STEWART: *(Looking around.)* Hey, where's Andy?

RANDALL: Probably communing with nature somewhere.

ROBIN: Ahhh ... my back is killing me.

RANDALL: I haven't been this stiff since I owned that stupid futon.

STEWART: Andy?? You out there?

RANDALL: Jeez, Stewart, let the guy relieve himself in peace.

ROBIN: Andy's pack is gone.

STEWART: What?

RANDALL: He couldn't have gone far. I mean it's not like he knows the way home.

ROBIN: I dunno. It was kind of a breakthrough for him last night. Maybe he just, you know, couldn't face us this morning.

RANDALL: Yeah, well, we're not exactly a pretty sight.

STEWART: Maybe he tried to go back alone.

RANDALL: Andy wouldn't leave us behind ... we're the four musketeers, right?

ROBIN: I thought we were the four stooges.

RANDALL: *(Pause.)* Yeah, well, that was yesterday. *(Goes over to ROBIN.)* Look, Robin, I guess I was being kind of a jerk.

ROBIN: Yeah, you were. *(Pause.)* So was I.

STEWART: What about me?

RANDALL: Okay. You're a jerk, too.

STEWART: Yesss!!

(They all laugh. ANDY enters, pack on his back.)

ANDY: Morning, guys.

STEWART: Where were you?

(ANDY opens the pack and takes out a large McDonald's bag. He starts pulling out Egg McMuffins, Hashbrowns, etc. The others look at him, paralysed.)

ANDY: It's a beautiful day, isn't it? Listen, I hope everyone likes Egg McMuffins. I figured you guys might be a little hungry so I got lots of these hashbrown things.

RANDALL: It's a mirage, Stewart. It'll pass.

ANDY: *(Opens an Egg McMuffin and waves it in front of the guys.)* Mmmm. It's real.

(The wild guys fall on the McDonald's bag like a pack of ravenous wolves.)

Turns out we camped a mile from the highway.

(The others all look up at him, stunned. Then they look at STEWART.)

It's interesting, isn't it? Being lost isn't a physical condition, it's a mental condition. If we had known yesterday, for example, …

RANDALL: Andy?

(RANDALL steps up to ANDY and smears ketchup on his face. ANDY is surprised for a moment, then squirts RANDALL back.)

ROBIN: The blood of the prey!

(STEWART and ROBIN get into the act and soon they're all smearing ketchup on their faces and doing The Dance of the Fast Food Products around the firepit. A group of friends at last.

Suggested music fades up: "Teach Your Children" by Crosby, Stills, Nash and Young. The end.)